About the Author

Mike Stubblefield, aka "Stubb", is a life-long waterman who has sailed, motored, airboated, poled and paddled the waters of Florida and offshore islands for many years. He is a free lance writer for various outdoor magazines such as "Sail" "On Shore/Off Shore" "Coastal Angler" "Paddler" and "Kayak Fishing" and others. In 2006, he published **"Confessions of a Fisherman & Other Lies."** He spends his time between a small place on Chokoloskee Island and near the banks of the St. Johns River in Sanford, Florida.

RULE # 13

A Chump in Chokoloskee

Fishing Tales of the Florida Backcountry

Mike Stubblefield

Copyright: Jack Michael Stubblefield 2008
All rights reserved.

ISBN: 978 – 0 – 615 – 25127 - 1
First Edition: October, 2008
Publisher: Jack Michael Stubblefield
Printed in the U.S.A.

Front & rear cover photographs courtesy of yours truly, Stubb.

For contact: stubb54@yahoo.com

Preface

I'm not from Chokoloskee; I'm a frequent visitor, some-time resident, observer and fisherman that would almost rather poke around the backcountry as actually catch a fish. When the bite is off, I'm probably half lost in some creek or mangrove tunnel wondering why my GPS isn't giving me the proper readout.

And, since I've lived in small communities of Florida and Texas, I know "if you aren't from there, you'll never be from there." That's fine. I want to tread lightly, leave a faint footprint, and not disturb the natives in their continual fight to keep condos, bulldozers and fast food joints out of their sight and out of the town limits.

Of course, your question is: **"What's Rule # 13?"** It's really quite simple and well-known but takes many forms. My favorite version is taken from a man called Uncle John; an old poacher and ranch hand that worked for me at a fish camp on the St Johns River. I quote him:

"If'n the fish're where they never was, then they ain't where they always was before."

And, a different approach to Rule # 13 would be:

"The fish're where I ain't."

Or, again:

"The fish are always somewhere else."

No matter which version of Rule #13 you like, it's a universal fact for all of us fisherfolk. At least it is for those of us who are not seen regularly on TV catching huge gamefish constantly with a big grin and with their very own official photographer to record history. .

At any rate, the collected tales here are not about anyone you've heard of .. they are short pieces that chronicle the experiences of my friends, myself and those we've encountered. You won't read of expert fisherfolk; you will read of hot days, running aground, getting skunked and learning Everglades lessons the hard way.

The characters are real people, the stories are all true. Well, maybe there's been some exageration here and there, but not a lot.

If I've offended anyone, sue me. Just get in line.

ms

An Overview of the 10,000 Islands and Chokoloskee

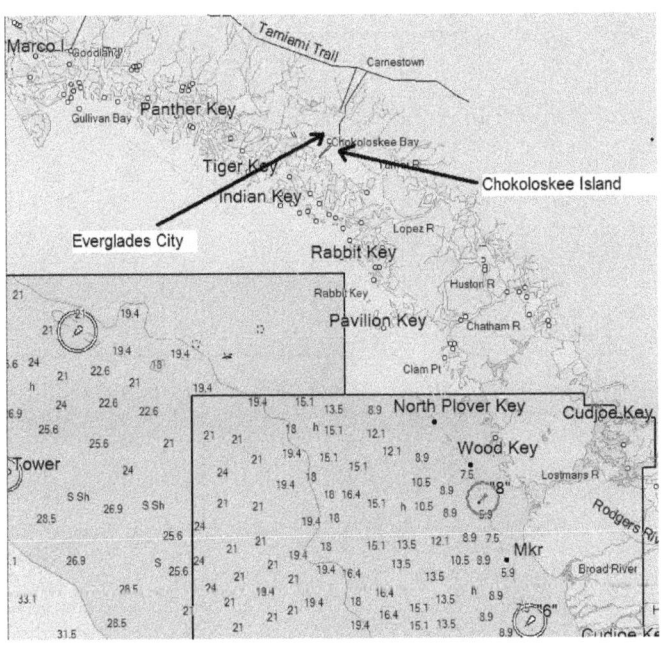

Gulf Coastal Everglades extends from Marco Island south to Cape Sable (not shown). Chokoloskee Island is in the middle of the maze of mangrove islets, sloughs, bayous and rivers known as the 10,000 Islands. Other than Marco Island (upper left), Everglades City & Chokoloskee, none of the keys or waterways are inhabited (that we know of).

Map courtesy of Garmin, Inc.; MapSource

Contents

Note: If you were looking for a rational, organized lay out, you're reading the wrong book. However, here are the general topics. Each topic will have several stories, essays or what I call "snapshots."

The Fine Art of Getting "There" in One Piece
Pages 11 – 37
Barhopping Chokoloskee
Chumps in Chokoloskee
Lostmans Luck
What's the Forecast?
Finding Your Way

Backcountry Camping
Pages 38 - 61
The $200 Cot
The Camp Lonesome Tango
The Willy Willy Option
The Wilderness at Low Water

Just Folks
Pages 63 - 81
The Bendback Beadbutt Baitfish
Dog Days Chickee Fishing
42 Degrees in the Shade

Small Craft Maintenance
Pages 83 - 98
Small Craft Maintenance I
Small Craft Maintenence II
Small Craft Maintenance III

Character(s)
Page 99

The Fine Art of Getting "There" in One Piece

I've been in, on, under or around boats of all sizes most of my life. One would think, after these years and experiences, that I have the lessons learned ingrained in my brain. But, that doesn't seem to be the case. I should have the lessons tatoo'd on my arms for quick reference. A printed, waterproof "rules" sheet would be handy but I'd just lose or misplace it.

I always say that any day spent on the water wherein I'm not cut, maimed or drowned has been a good one.

Read on....

Bar Hopping at Chokoloskee

A number of years ago I swore off using engines after making a mini fish reef by throwing a British made outboard off the transom of a rented skiff. You note I said "throwing" and not "losing" the motor. Thing would run for about ten seconds and croak. I likened that motor to a gas operated blender and the only difference, really, was that at least the blender has a reverse. Anyhow, in a fit of frustrated rage, I unscrewed the bolts, lifted and heaved it over the side with great satisfaction.

I've spent the last seven or eight years kayak fishing and and enjoy it immensely even though I discovered a whole new set of rules to fish by. I won't go into those rules as I've published the first thirteen of them previously; and, now, I've got nearly three hundred and fifty rules and plan publishing them as soon as I can afford a full ream of paper.

However, the desire to wander further and faster than a kayak allows bit me this year and I found myself the owner of new 15' mini skiff with an elderly but serviceable fifteen horse motor. Wide and stable, has a platform, can tow my kayak to distant places and moves fast enough to get on a plane. It was time to explore regions that would take hours, if not days, by paddle craft.

And so it was that friend Gator hooked up his air conditioned pop top camper and I hooked up the little skiff and we roared south to Chokoloskee Island armed with Blue Nav charts for the GPS, a tarpon rod each, and a memory of previous kayaking trips to the 10,000 Islands. Gator, eyeballing the '78 model motor, opted to take his kayak, too, because,as he said: "I want to get back to Choko, understand…?" Boy's got no faith at all.

Our only motoring experience in that region was on the kayak mothership of Captain Charles Wright. We spent two days a year ago in the back country and Cap'n Chuck managed to hit nothing … I mean not even an overhanging mangrove limb .. in his 27' skiff. I had visions of doing the same, you see.

Our first day of fishing we had the good luck to meet up with good friend Vivian Oliva who has years of experience in the Islands. She mapped out the passes, short cuts rarely used except by locals, spotted us good fishing holes, printed out the tide charts and all but patted us on the head. Gator and Vivian took off on their kayaks and while they fished Chokoloskee Bay, I zipped the skiff out what I'll call "Viv's Pass" and seven miles later was drift fishing near Demijohn Key. And caught some nice trout, too!! And, more importantly, I had a good low tide GPS track to follow back since I hadn't hit a single oyster on my way out.

"How tough could this be?" I gloated.

The return trip was successful .. no "hard aground" … no scrapes on the hull .. no hiccups at all. I sauntered up to what we called "The Veranda", an open air roofed patio down by the camp ground's docks, and joined everyone to swap tales, lies and universal truths. Several experienced fisherman questioned me on my first solo and I nonchalantly passed it off as not a big deal.

I was pushing my luck but didn't know it. The tip off the next day would be different came about 9p.m. when Choko got nearly four inches of rain in less than an hour. A very small mini skiff with no bilge fills quickly and had it not been low tide and the bow resting in mud, the trip would have been done. An hour of frantic bailing cleaned her up but it was touch and go.

Day two. Well, let me summarize it this way. Gator and I motored out of the tiny marina and hit a sand bar within ten seconds. We got free of that, motored the three hundred yards to Smallwood's Store and found an unseen oyster bed. After some cussing and fumbling, we got off and headed for Choko Pass following my track of the previous day, naturally. I think some demon moved the GPS track because although we stayed dead on it, we hopped into half a dozen more oyster bars with fine precision. Gator created a waypoint on each one of them but complained his GPS was about out of waypoint memory.

Finally, we got into the more open waters of the Pass and at full throttle I made gradual turn, again right on track, and a hand clenching "KEEERACK .. WHANNNNGGG" sound came from the motor, which died, and we sat there in silence and stared at one another.

"Stubb, you must've shaved that turn back there a bit too much, huh?"

"Naw, man .. I was right on it….I wonder if we still have a prop .. do you see the lower unit anywhere? It's white like the head you know…"

I leaned over the poling platform and yanked the motor up. No paint and no chipped prop? Lower unit in tact? I couldn't believe it. And the motor fired right up and zoomed us straight into a nearby sand bar.

Some one was moving these bars over night, I knew it.

But, we made it to Rabbit and Lumber Key and did some fishing. Gator lost a monster snook; we caught some trout and enjoyed ourselves; and managed to stay afloat that morning. On our return, we ventured up into Rabbit Key Pass and felt pretty smug as we followed a homeward bound boat that obviously knew the lay of the bars.

I got too confident, though. Right near the entrance to the Lopez River this boat did what appeared to be a 270 degree turn within a space of fifty feet and at full speed. I blinked, tried to duplicate the manuever, but it was too late .. yessiree, Bubbas; we were hard aground once again.

By my count Gator and I discovered 38 new bars in or near Chokoloskee Island in three days of fishing. These are oyster bars not frequented by many fishermen and I can recommend them all as being instantly accessible and downright welcoming to anyone with a new skiff.

Oh, yeah … I had to get a new prop but the paint was gone off the original one anyhow.

Chumps in Chokoloskee

Some fishing trips are amazingly trouble free, successful ventures out on to Florida's waterways complete with great tales, action packed pictures, and memories of big fish. Then there are my trips which tend to fall into the "survivor" category of near-misses, bad timing, unexpected gear failure and emergency first aid lessons. If I were to catalog my forays down into the Everglades, most of them would fall mid way between "disaster" and "moderately successful." Of course, "moderately successful," by my set of rules, means all hands got ashore under their own power and, after a few cold beverages and when the shock wore off, could laugh about the events.

Not long ago I was talking about a trip taken a year or so back wherein we caught a large number of snook but fought rough bays, came close to being swamped, ran out of gas in the back country, fought mosquitos the size of eagles and so on. My listeners, a couple whose only experience of fish was seeing them in the supermarket, stared at me in silence. Then they asked: "So you do those trips for fun?"

Right after I bought my micro skiff, named The Rule #13, Gator and I loaded up his pop-top camper and highballed straight to Chokoloskee Island. We set-up camp at the Island RV Park on the western shore. Our first day, we made systematic discoveries of numerous slightly submerged oyster bars within sight of Choko; and then somehow made it out to Rabbit Key, fished, got skunked, and limped home before the inevitable summer thunder boomers arrived. We snugged the skiff up in her slip and joined the other sunblasted fishermen in the chickee to exchange lies and sip ice cold Cuba Libres.

About dinner time, Gator and I strolled to the camper to sit out a storm brewing and enjoy the air conditioning. The rain that hit the island was your typical Florida frog strangler: the wind howled, it rained incredibly hard, and the camper shook like it was riding out an earthquake as Gator and I mixed a few more Libres. In mid-sip, Gator asked:

"Stubb, you ever mount a bilge pump?"
"No. I decided to keep it minimalist, you know? No fancy stuff .. no wiring to mess with. Just the trolling motor," I replied with smug self-satisfaction. "I got a bucket layin' in the bilge."

"Hmmph. May need it this keeps up. Lemme check the weather channel…"

NOAA's cyborg-voiced report advised we were getting a four inch per hour monsoon. We looked at each other and I knew what was going through Gator's head.

"Stubb. I figure at four inches per hour, an' we been sittin' in here almost an hour, the volume of yer boat's about half filled. 'Member, you only got eight'r nine inches a' freeboard."
"Nah," I yawned, "she's fine…."

At that moment the down pour stopped as suddenly as it started and someone was pounding on the camper's tin and canvas door. Gator opened up and we heard:

"Buddy, that little shalla water skiff's yours, ain't it? Yeah? Well she's 'bout sunk. Tide's out so the bow's sittin' on oysters but them gas tanks is gonna float to Everglades City purty quick."

Fortunately it was low tide and the motor was still above water. With the bow hard aground I could stand forward and was able to bail further and further aft as I developed bucket elbow. I rationalized that it was nice, fresh rain water so the skiff had been de-salted and was quite clean.

That evening we drove into Naples and I picked up a bilge pump. Not automatic, mind you, since that went against my "minimalist" mentality. It was just a straight "hook it up and she pumps" kind of rig. Gator, in a fit of self-preservation, bought a hand operated pump that he justified as back-up. As he laid it on the counter, I asked him:

"What's that for? I got what we need right here?"
"Yeah, but it ain't installed and knowin' you it'll sit in the storage well under half a zillion things an' nowhere near the battery."

Guy can get irritating at times even though he's a good friend.

The next morning we were up before daylight, motor idling, tuning the GPS, checking a chart by flashlight and plotting our course for Lost Man's Creek. We'd been advised juvenile tarpon were rolling around in plenty and we aimed to stake our claim to some. When there was just enough light to see, we took off and promptly discovered several oyster bars that had increased in size during the night. But, we make it through with the lower unit scarred but intact.

For those not familiar with the coastal Everglades and the Wilderness Waterway, it's a series of interconnected bays, rivers, creeks and mangrove tunnels that winds southeasterly and vaguely towards the ranger station at Flamingo. There are sections where the Waterway is a narrow neck between islets. If two boats meet head on it can get tight. One such spot is near Alligator Creek. We hadn't seen another boat in an hour and I slowed a bit as we approached one of those narrow passes to check my GPS and make sure it was where I wanted to go. Right then, a twenty two foot bay boat rounded the bend headed for the pass and backed off his speed as he passed me. Only trouble with slowing down was that as his stern settled it increased his wake to a size about quadruple my skiff's freeboard. He waved and smiled and we took on blue water over the side as I had no room to manuever.

I killed the motor and we sloshed up into the mangroves, which, of course, necessitated digging out our mosquito netting. We had to move very carefully since hurried movement might put more water into the boat.

"Stubb?" mumbled Gator as he pulled a headnet on, "where's that pump?"
"Ummm, err, Hmm." I thought for a moment. "In the back of the pick-up?"

Gator just sighed and snatched the bailing bucket as it floated by him.

Lostmans Luck

As usual, I was a bit less than half lost since I'd let my GPS batteries die, and the waterproof chart aboard took a swim back in Chevalier Bay. I'd been counting the bays and narrow creeks ticking the names off mentally, but then got distracted by running into a sandbar in a narrow pass right before Plate Creek. Now I couldn't recall if this was Lostmans or Two Island or Onion Key Bay and was beating my brain trying to recall if we'd gone through three or four of the little creeks on the northern section of the Wilderness Waterway. The obvious way to find out our location was to look for the camping chickee along Lostmans northern shore. We looked. It wasn't there. Hmm. I slowed to an idle while we swept the mangroves looking for some dimly recalled landmark which is tough to do when there's a hundred miles of similar looking terrain.

"Well, we gotta be in either ..."
"Either which, Les?" I prompted. "Remember, the reason we've come this far is to jump some baby tarpon in Tom's Creek. So it's kinda important to pinpoint where we are and get to Lostmans River, you know?"
"Yeah, yeah. And who forgot charged batteries and didn't tape the chart down, huh?"
I sighed: "Guilty; but you coulda been holdin' on to the chart, hombre."
"I was busy makin' sure the beer was iced down..."

Les and I received valuable human intelligence the night before while sitting and swatting mosquitoes in the RV park's chickee. Two fishermen, later vouched for as "reliable" by the park's manager, went on at great length about the fun they had catching ten to fifteen pound tarpon and snook in Tom's Creek. Since our day produced a total skunk, we were eager and interested listeners. Tom's was a goodly run for my mini-skiff; it would total nearly twenty six miles one way running inside. The outside route, out in the Gulf, was not an option given the predicted SSW winds over fifteen knots. We couldn't resist. We left Chokoloskee at first light the next morning.

Eventually we stumbled on to Lostmans River since I vaguely recalled that the Waterway marker number fifty two was the turnoff. I steered for the river and when we reached it started doubling back along the south shore looking for Tom's Creek. The creek meanders a good distance from Lostmans, around a large mangrove key, sidesteps a nameless bay, then heads into the interior 'Glades. It looked quiet, deep, and, importantly, very fishy and "tarponish." With the incoming tide, we drifted the creek using the trolling motor to nudge the skiff's course.

"Not much activity, is there..?" Les said with his voice muffled by his mosquito headnet.
"Should be some snook 'round here but keep your eyes open for tarpon rolling," I told him.

About right then, Les and I both hooked snook on our small gold and chartreuse plastic lures. Both snook were in the twenty four inch size; not giants, but fun on light tackle. This size snook seemed to be all around us nestled down in the murky, muddy waters where Tom's Creek steps briefly into that shallow, nameless side bay. For once, I decided not to leave fish to find fish, and we each caught several snook during the next hour.

But where were all the tarpon so lavishly described the night before? We eased around the bay in front of the area where Tom's dives into the mangroves again; and, out of the corner of my eye, I saw a dark fin and silvery side briefly surface.

"Tarpon!" I croaked. "And again, over there; maybe fifty yards. Use the pole, not the troller, Les!" I muttered as I clambered up on the platform trying to juggle rod and pushpole. Les was so startled at my yelps and quick moves that he dropped a beer bottle on the deck. It sounded like a cannon shot:

"Dadblastit, man! Gotta be quiet 'round these fish!" I whispered loud enough to startle a great blue heron nearby.
"Sorry, sorry .. " and he tiptoed to his rod and cast blindly.

And immediately hooked a thrashing, leaping, gill rattling tarpon of about twelve pounds. Les whooped and hollered. I wanted to cast also but was too busy getting a treble hook out of my shirt tail. By the time I just ripped the hook loose in complete frustration, Les had releasd his tarpon, threw again, and had a second one.

"Stubb! Get a picture of this one for me!" Les yelled as the fish went airborne a fourth time.
"You got a camera in your pocket and I don't recall bein' your official photographer.."

However, in the spirit of comradeship, I climbed down off the platform, fumbled for the camera, got it ready and the tarpon spit the hook.

"OK. My turn, bubba. You get up there and pole."

Les didn't argue and he poled… and poled. And I cast my arm off at rolling tarpon for the next hour but the silver devils weren't having it. All the while, Les was talking to himself about what a fine day it turned out to be .. his snook, *his* tarpon. I say he was talking to himself because my jaw was jacked shut and I was ignoring him.

After my two hundredth cast at those fun-loving, lolling and lazily rolling tarpon, I sat down on the cooler and popped a top. I used the cold bottle to replace the sweat on my face and contemplated the injustice of the universe.

Les glanced at the sky and said: "Getting' on to thunderboomer time, Stubb. Maybe we should think about heading back to Choko?"

"Yup. Wouldn't want to disturb all these fish around here. Probably too distracted to muster up a laugh. Besides, I ripped my best fishin' shirt with this treble hook here."

"Too bad you didn't hook a poon, Stubb" Les mumbled.

"Mmmf" I responded as I chugged an ice cold beer.

As I cranked the motor, Les was lifting the troller up, and we were both watching the ocassional juvenile tarpon roll. With motor at idle, I stood up, put a hand on the grab bar and scanned the shallow bay waters looking for a channel. Right at that moment, a tarpon came over my shoulder and landed at Les' feet. We were too stunned to move as the fish nearly beat itself to pieces hitting every rod and reel and tackle box.

Les grabbed the fish with the gripper and held it up:

"Seven pounder, Stubb! Got your tarpon. Lostman's luck!"

"What's the Forecast?"

Over the years I've relied on any number of websites, local TV and radio stations, local wisemen and magicians to help me with the weather. I've chronicled some of those experiences in other articles. What I've found, essentially, is that there are prevailing weather conditions that coincide with the months of the year here in east central Florida. However, the named months, e.g. "February" or "March," do not always adequately bring to mind what a fisherman will face in that particular month.

For instance, recently my Atlanta friend Tacklehead called to set up a visit with me to Chokoloskee.

Tack had not been down this way in over a year and his local weather memory was obviously rusty:

"Stubb, how 'bout the end of April? Few showers, some afternoon breezes, huh?"

"No, Tack. You fergit. It's still March."

"No it ain't, it's the middle of April; look at yer calendar!"

"Don't need to, Tack. It's March conditions."

There was a puzzled silence on the other end of the cell phone connection.

So, you see? "April," in Tacklehead's mind brought up visions of really nice days with, oh, a shower here and there .. maybe need a waterproof shirt or jacket, pleasant temperatures and bearable humidity. He, like most folks, thinking of "April," had a complete disconnect with reality.

After that conversation I got to thinking about the months' nomenclature and decided to do something about it. I located the only working ball point pen in my house and some paper, set a $5 plastic chair on the balcony overlooking my skiff and kayak under the huge old oak tree, and set to work

First, I reasoned, there are three seasons in south Florida best described as:

1. Windy; cool (November, December, January, February)
2. Windy, mild (March, April, October)
3. Hurricane-ish, hot and humid (May, June, July, August, September)

With that knowledge, and using the names of three months that bring up images burned in our collective folklore, you could rename them all thusly (keeping my list above in mind):

1. December A, December B, December C, December B
2. March A, March B, March C
3. July A, July B, July C, July D, July E

But that was cumbersome, after all. I could envisage a conversation like this with Tacklehead:

"How bout I come down middle of next month, Stubb?"

"Well, Tack, that'd put you here 'bout July B, 15th to the 20th, right?"

"Huh?"

So, back to my note pad and balcony; and, since it was after high noon, I figured a chilled bottle of anything would help the thought processes a great deal. I reasoned that the whole US of A would recognize the name "March" as a seasonal word bringing to mind "WIND." Good enough. July brings thoughts of heat and possible big storms; and, I scrapped grouping #1 (December as a major indicator) since "March" would cover that wind image. Couple all this with a general idea of temperatures, humidity levels and tropical storm threats associated with other months, and it would work. Thus, after my sixth chilled bottle, I came up with the following:

JanuMar; FebruMar, March, ApriMar, JuliMay, JuliJune, July, JuliAug, JuliSept OctiMar, NoveMar, DeceMar.

A few minutes into this, I ran to the store and secured another case of pre-chilled bottles and while doing this errand, another idea popped up. Every fisherman in southwest Florida knows that during the Winter months, December and January in particular, the water can be low given that the north winds blow the water out of the bays and rivers. Ah, ha! I'd add a small syllable to help with that image. Thus, I changed DeceMar and JunuMar to:

DeceloMar and JanuloMar.

I must say I was pleased with myself. I very much liked the sound of some of the months; JuliMay reminded me of a girl I once dated back in Texas long ago. JuliSept had sort of a noble Romano-Latin ring to it and I really was fond of DeceloMar.

I immediately got on the phone to call up an attorney friend of mine, who is also a fishing buddy, to get some information on copyrights for my revolutionary calendar, forgetting that it was now nearly midnight. He wasn't exactly thrilled with the call and assumed I was in jail and needed bail.

"Stubb, I don't think you can copyright this, and why bother?" he yawned

"Whaddya mean, Rev? Sure I can. You can copyright a particular calendar, right?"

"Yeah, you can the 'content' of the calendar if the images and such are yours; but the month names?"

"We'll be rich, Rev. Last time this was done, it was the during the French Revolution!"

"Yup," said the Rev; "And look at all the good it done them." And he hung up on me.

Well, it's been over a month now since my idea was firmed up into something solid and I'm still out there marketing the Stubborian Weather Indicator

Calendar. I've got Google Ads running looking for venture capital; I got an on-line website to print me up some samples, and I'm taking them to tackle shops and marinas and talking to fishermen everywhere I go.

Just the other day, I ran into FrenchFly and Half-Naked Charley while visiting up near Titusville.

"Say, Stubb, when you headed back down to Chokoloskee?" asked Charley.

"'Bout mid JuliJune, I think. Had to cancel my JuliMay trip. If I don't make it down there then it might have to wait 'til DeceloMar," I sighed.

"Huh?"

Finding Your Way

A long number of years ago, I started sailing with friends that circumnavigated Florida's coastal waters. Primarily, we used "dead reckoning" with the aid of paper charts, a fixed steering compass, a hand bearing compass and a pair of binoculars to sight landmarks. Many an hour was spent down in the galley, hunkered over the table, plotting a course from bearings taken, then yelling course corrections to the person at the helm.

Once in a while, a sailor would have a radio direction finder (RDF). This was a neat gizmo that dated back many decades. Basically, you had a radio with a bearing compass and large gun sight that was mounted on the RDF. You tuned in Radio Havana, for instance, or "equis y doble u" (XEW) in Mexico City and then some country western station along the Florida coast. You simply triangulated these three signals and pinpointed where you were. It worked great IF (a big "if") you were in radio reception range.

Then along came LORAN. Wow. All us salty waterfolk were impressed. The gizmo let you tune into LORAN transmitting stations scattered up and down the coast and you got a very exact position reading. This ranked right up there with the new handheld calculators, car-mounted mobile phones, and other wonders of the world. It, too, worked well unless you ventured far off shore and ran out of signal reception; then, it was back to dead reckoning.

About 1994, I believe, I saw my first handheld Global Positioning System (GPS) unit. This rig let you input lattitude and longitude as waypoints and would indicate if you were on or off course. There were no map graphics available then but the data made life easier on dark nights in unfamiliar waters. You could depart from Riviera Beach at midnight; sail across to the The Rock north of Grand Bahama; arrive before dawn and have some comfort knowing the Gulf Stream was not sending you to Iceland or Newfoundland.

There could be problems, of course, and a wise waterman always plotted his course by dead reckoning, along with the GPS, as a back up safety plan. The importance of this became apparent to me in 1995, at two in the morning, as the boat I was aboard approached Green Turtle and the GPS' batteries died. And, nearly six hours earlier during ship's happy hour, we'd forgotten to keep track of our progress on the charts. We dropped anchor in order to stand still, and finally found spare batteries buried under a hundred cases of emergency beverage rations (read: "beer"). Fortunately, the GPS saved its data and we made it in without grinding our keel on a coral head.

It took me another decade to get a GPS, which now had amazing graphics, maps and a zillion other features, all loaded on to a memory card ready to insert in the GPS. When venturing out on my kayak or mini skiff, I'd know exactly where I was. This thing also had an alarm that reminded me I was lost every 15 seconds. But, I discovered, if I really wanted good maps and info for the salty waterways, I'd need to get the right GPS software: Blue Nav charts and the like. Pricey, but an incredible tool for a boatman.

So, I went on the internet, to GPS manufacturer "XYZ," and tried to order a graphics card. I was completely puzzled by their shopping cart and after a frustrating hour I located a real phone number and called "Sales," which I noted was located in San LaLaLand, California. The call went something like this:

(Music while on hold: "Darth Vader's March" from "Star Wars, Ch. 1")
(Music stops, then sounds like someone fumbling with a headset, followed by a deep exhaled breath. The sound a smoker makes after a satisfying hit.)

"Hey, good morning! Thanks for calling XYZ Nav Systems and my name's …."(?).
"What was your name again, m'am?"
"Jaqi."
"You spell that J A C K I E?"
"No! That's so like last century, you know. I spell it J A Q I." she tittered and exhaled noisily again.
"OK, got it. I want to order your memory card with a Florida Blue Nav chart."
(another exhale, cough, and a sigh)
"Scuse me, but, like, what was that again?" (sound of headset moved away from mouth)
"I wanta order XYZ's Blue Nav memory card. Your website says you've got a 10% discount on accessories. That discount work on this order?"

"Hahahahaha! Oh, no, man. Like, a Blue Nav chart's not an accessory; it's a necessity!"

"Well, yeah, you're right. So I want it and what do we need to do next, Jaqi?"

"Hmmm. (sigh). Guess I need some cash first, huh?"

"OK, Jaqi, I'll need you to email me a receipt, please" (this after the credit card information was passed on.).

"A what? Email? Oh, I don't know, man; it's like these people are so paranoid about viruses and stuff, but, like, gimme it anyway. The email address."

"Jaqi; when can I expect shipment and with which carrier?"

"Pigeon! Hahahaha! No, like, I think we use ExFed or whatever, you know? 'Bout five days? Zorantha in back here programs the Nav cards and she's like totally way cool. You can call back for the ExFed number, OK?"

"You'll email me, right, Jaqi?"

"Mmmmm; like I'll talk to Zorantha 'bout that, you know?"

I had some misgivings but five days later I had my chart on a card and, surprise, got a call from XYZ's Miz Jaqi doing a customer service follow-up:

"Say, Mr Stubb, like you did get your charts, right? Goody!

How'm I doin'? Oh, wow, like it's a totally down day here, man. Every one including Zorantha is grumpy and, you know?"

However, that conversation was short since I was out on the salt, easing along with my loaded up

GPS, looking for fish and marking holes known only to maybe five thousand other fishermen.

No time for Jaqi.

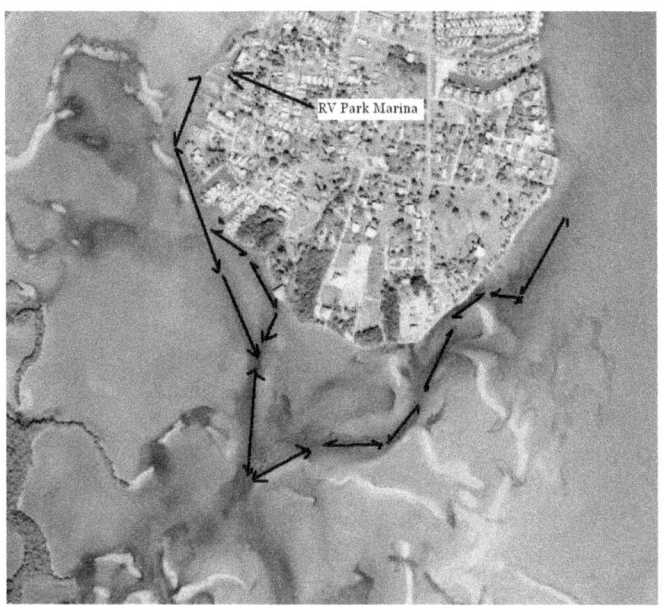

(Note: the above aerial shows Chokoloskee Island's southern shore and the boat killing oyster bars laying in wait just below the water.)

Backcountry Camping

At one time I was married to a young lady who considered "roughing it" to be staying in a hotel with no mall nearby. The older I get, the more I think she had it right. However, I still do it, and most times enjoy it as well.

The one thing about camping, particularly in the subtropics, is that you never know what you're gonna get. You can plan, pack, and consider every eventuality but without fail, if the bugs are bad, you'll leave the repellant, or if camped on a shell mound your Thermarest mattress is in a friend's garage. I have a "rule" about that and need to write it down.

The one thing I have learned: you don't plan a camping trip in mid-summer. I can remember that rule.

The $200 Cot

No Motor Zone Ned stood on the battered dock next to a Chokoloskee Island launch ramp and rubbed his bearded chin as he eyeballed the loaded skiffs. Each carried multiple jerry cans of fuel, boxes of camping gear, grub and tackle. There wasn't a spare inch of bare deck in sight and you could tell his orderly, engineering oriented brain was calculating weight, load and boat draft and how that would effect gas consumption in the planned Everglades loop trip.

There were three skiffs: my 15' Riverhawk powered by a 15hp Johnson; Gator's Gheenoe Classic rocket ship pushed with a 25hp Yamaha; and NMZ Ned's brand new 15' G3 aluminum jon boat sporting a 20hp 4 stroke electric start. The plan was to run 45 miles south that January day down to Camp Lonesome and explore the back country. After two nights at Lonesome, we'd venture back north to Camp Willy Willy and then make the long run home up the Wilderness Waterway. All this depended, of course, on whether the mild weather would hold. If a big nor'wester were to hit, and dried up the back country, then we'd be faced with a a run along the Gulf Islands in unfriendly chop in very small boats. Having been in that situation in the Everglades a year earlier, Gator and I knew it was something we didn't want to repeat. Twenty knot winds, NNW, caused us to creep along, pole and grunt our way the 17 miles from Darwin's Place back to Chokoloskee. It was a four hour endurance contest.

"Well, Stubb, think we got it all? What we need?" asked Ned.
"Believe so ... lessee, here: spare prop, you got the tools; gallon a' water per day per person; tents, fleece sleeping bags, grub's in that truck box; here's mine 'n Gator's cots .. where's your cot, Ned?"
"Right here in this plastic grocery bag," replied Ned as he rummaged through the stuff piled on his foredeck.
"That's a cot?" Gator blurted out. "In that tiny bag?"
"Yupperee. Mylar, plastic and collapsible rods like tent poles. Weighs two pound 'n floats your tail 'bout four inches off the ground. Latest high tech campin' doodad. Bit costly but I aim to sleep good."

We didn't have time to discuss this marvel of engineering, so the Micro Skiff Fishing Fleet set sail south. We wound our way through the Turner River, Hurdles Creek, and then skimmed our way through shallow bays and mangrove tunnel creeks along the Wilderness Waterway. We passed a fisherman or two and the ocassional paddling group; we took a break at Lostman's, then at the Rodger's River chickee where we checked charts and GPS' for the Broad River turn off to Camp Lonesome. By the time we meanedered through Alligator and Plate Creeks, we'd left the last of people and boats behind. We saw not another person the next two days.

By the time we arrived at Camp Lonesome, after driving most of the night to Chokoloskee, launching, then running the Waterway all morning, then setting up camp, we were bushed. However, Gator and I revived somewhat while we watched NMZ Ned unravel his new cot.

"Never did say how much you paid fer that thing, Ned.." I hinted.
"Was considerable," mumbled Ned as he set the small pieces and parts on a table and eyed the assembly instruction.
"How considerable, c'mon," asked Gator.
"Well, I got a discount cuz I'm a member of a fly club, you see, but, er, ummm, I think it was 'bout two hundred with shipping….." Ned responded in a low voice.

Gator and I were stunned:

"Two hundred Yankee dollars?" I needed clarification on this.
"Er, uh huh. Yup. Pretty close to it…"
"Does that cot play music? Have a heater? Does it mix drinks?" Gator exclaimed.

But Ned ignored us and quickly put the cot together, an amazing puzzle of small rings and poles and mylar. The cot stood, indeed, about 4 inches off the ground. We tested it out for sag … and the mylar "bed" didn't give hardly at all. Ned, satisfied with the construct, lifted up his one man tent, set it on top of the cot, and pegged the tent in place.

"Nap time," Ned stated with smug satisfaction as he crawled in and started snoring immediately.

Our weather held, temperatures in the high 70s, calm windless mornings and breezy wouth winds in the afternoons. We explored eastwards into freshwater creeks off the Broad and Wood Rivers and found a back country nameless lagoon filled with every kind of fish except the big he-monster snook.

In that lagoon, NMZ Ned saw a tarpon roll and lobbed a shallow running hard plug to it. I heard him yell: "Wow! Tarpon on!!!!!" and as I turned my skiff around witnessed a big tarpon go airborne. The next eight minutes Ned's G3 was towed by that leaping fish and I did my best to snap a picture of it in the air but wasn't fast enough. Finally, the tarpon jumped again near Ned, and snapped the hooks off the treble. It looked like wire cutters had done their job on that plug.

But, we all agreed that we would count that a "catch" given the length of time on and the fact that the tarpon was nearly boated. Ned's trip, he claimed, was already a success.

"Not ever day you hook up with a monster like that .. particularly on a flat calm day in a back country lagoon that looks like it's on another planet," Ned said. "An' that there cot was worth ever penny. I'll see if I can get you boys my discount if you want…."

The Camp Lonesome Tango

After running the roughly fifty miles from Chokoloskee Island south along the Wilderness Waterway, No Motor Zone Ned, Gator and I pulled up to the tiny dock at Camp Lonesome. The dock with a bright blue porta-potti was all we could see other than a very narrow tunneled walkway through the mangoves.

"Hoo-boy," whistled Gator. "Pray the bugs're takin' a Winter nap!"
"Oh, my ever-lovin'….." Ned mumbled as he realized his headnet was still in the truck many miles away.
"Well, Gator, at least that blue potti matches your Crocs an' visor exactly," was my response.

We strolled up the dock, long sleeves buttoned, bug jackets zipped, and two of the three of us wearing precious head netting. We stopped in the middle of the small jungle clearing, listened for the buzz, heard nothing, and slowly, just like space explorers who realize the atmosphere of a strange planet was breathable, removed protective layers.

Like most of the coastal Everglades' dry land camp sites, Lonesome was a shell mound surrounded with thick growing mangroves, gumbo limbo, buttonwood and every manner of scrub. The vegetation forms a near impenetrable (for humans!) wall around a cleared area just big enough to allow three groups of campers to set up. We had the site to ourselves for the duration of our stay. In fact, we saw not another soul for two days. Once I thought I heard a boat motor off in the distance, but I wasn't sure.

Camp Lonesome is well inland from the coast on the Broad River and sits on the boundary of salt and freshwater creeks and lagoons. Our plan was to explore both waters. The only difficulty? Which of the dozens of fishy looking waterways to explore. However, shortly after our arrival, and following unloading cans of fuel, food, tents and related gear, setting up camp, and giving ourselves a sit-down break, fishing became a secondary thought.

"Man, after getting up at 2 a.m., driving 230 miles, loading, launching, running 50 miles, then doin' all this camp stuff, I'm a done-in bear," I moaned. "Gettin' old Stubb. Why, not long ago you'd already be out nosin' into that creek over there and hookin' your first mangrove tree," observed Gator.

"That well may be," I whipped back. "but my eyes're open right now and yours ain't, whippersnapper," and Gator, comfy in his canvas chair, began to snore.

Leaving youth to guard the camp site, NMZ Ned and I each picked a creek and took off. We wound through miles of little tributaries, some dead end, others going who knew where. Our handheld GPS' were of little value here as we were well off the charts. The GPS would, however, give you a cookie crumb trail to find your way home. We caught jacks, sighted snook in the 'grove roots, Ned reported via VHF he was surrounded by rolling gar and, thereby, must be in freshwater. Finally, exhausted, we returned to find a busy, bustling, officious and organizing Gator.

"Ned, I moved yer $200 cot an' tent over there since you set it up in a depression. It'd fill up with water if it rains. Stubb, I put your gas cans yonder out of reach of a smolderin' cigarette butt. I've got things set up to do dinner, now, so who's bartender?"

"Guess me, Sergeant Gator," and I started poking around for The Fisherman's Friend, a nicely aged half gallon of Barbados rum.

While doing that, Gator was busy ordering Ned around .. advising him of the correct flame setting for a fry pan and the optimal width of potato slices for cooking all the while ignoring the fact that NMZ Ned was something of a renowned camp chef. They had a mild disagreement about onions but I ignored that and instead savored my Caribbean rum. Dinner got cooked without any fist fights, and just after dark we were a hang-dog tired bunch. It was an early night.

Whipped though we all were, I spent a restless time in the tent. Ultimately, about 3 a.m. some scuffling noises alongside the tent got me out and into the absolute pitch black night. The only illumination was the stars shining through the occasional break in the overhead canopy of trees. I flashed a light around thinking to spook a hungry raccoon, but found nothing. Chilly, I grabbed a blanket and collapsed into my canvas chair and half dozed. Again, I heard a sliding, brushy noise. Near the tent again? No, I couldn't locate the source, and soon gave it up.

Just before dawn, something again woke me up. By now the blanket was heavy with dew, and I was half soaked and *really* awake. Earlier, I'd done my best not to wake everyone up, but it was coffee time and my banging around brought Ned to life and then Gator staggered into the lantern light and he immediately took over coffee chores. I let him.

"Mmmmph," snuffled Gator, "sinuses stopped up. What was that movin' 'round the tent last night?"
"Dunno. Put more sugar in that cup, willya?" I mumbled. "Ned, you havin' some, aren't ya? Say, how'd yer $200 cot sleep?"
"Good; howsomever, I may just warm up a cuppa that rum to get the kinks out."

Right about then, when Ned said the word "kinks," all two hundred pounds and six foot four inches of Gator jumped straight up in the air with a yell. The yell was sort of a mixture of "yikes!" "yipe!" "oooooww!" and several cuss words all blended together. He was standing on the picnic table bench by an act of levitation, then back off it before I could blink my eye.

"What the Hell…?" I sputtered through boiling coffee,
"Lookee there!!" Yelled Gator and pointed to a five foot long, fat, slithering eastern diamondback rattler moseying out from under the tent, by Gator's spot at the table and into the brush.
"Doggone, Gator; I didn't know you could dance!" laughed Ned who was busy pursuing the snake with a length of stick. "He's just looking for warmth, no harm, none at all….."

A bit later a somewhat grumpy Gator was explaining his behavior:

"Just surprised me half asleep as I was, you know…"

"Funny," I said. "I thought you was demonstrating the Camp Lonesome Tango fer me'n Ned. I enjoyed it, too, even though you didn't have a pretty partner."

I got no response to that but, it was still very early in the day.

The Willy Willy Option

Gator, No Motor Zone Ned and I got a late start leaving Camp Lonesome and there were two very good reasons for that. Firstly, Ned had eggs, sausage, onions and potatos that begged to be whipped into a fine breakfast. And, secondly, we had to return to our big, backwoods lagoon before we loaded up the camping gear, fuel and water. This lagoon, on the edge of the freshwater Everglades tributaries, was where Ned hooked, fought and after seven or eight minutes lost a huge tarpon. Over breakfast, the conversation went something like this:

"Stubb, sure glad you got some pictures even though they ain't too good. Leastwise I got proof I had that critter on a while."

"Ned those are valuable visual digital evidence. Better'n any independent, unbiased, third party witness of which we've got none around here," I told Ned.

"Well, I didn't see the tarpon," groused Gator around a mouthful of eggs and sausage, "but I consider myself to be fairly unbiased and trustworthy...." A statement that was greeted by howls of laughter.

However, we found no tarpon that morning. We did get into some hungry jacks and trout for a couple of hours but the wind kicked up mid-morning and we cut the lagoon visit short. We needed to move our base on to Camp Willy Willy before the wind churned the big bays to our north into lumpy, choppy messes. Our small skiffs are sturdy things but they don't like rough water and very little water over the sides can cause concern. This is particularly the case when, like me, you've neglected to mount an automatic bilge pump.

Fortunately for us, the wind was WSW 10-15 and gave us no difficulty other than some wet shirts as we crossed Rodgers River Bay. We'd seen not a soul in three days, but when we rounded an islet at Park marker 38, our turn-off for Rocky Creek, we were facing four large canoes full of bedraggled and rather forlorn looking trekkers. They waved paddles at us in a rather frantic way. Since I was the lead boat, and I thought the paddle waving meant they needed help, I idled over to them.

"You in trouble?" I called.

"Oh, no sir! Just wanted to make sure you didn't run us down," responded a man in a t-shirt that read "GUIDE."
"Well, course I wasn't gonna run you over!" I sputtered; but, then manners took over and I asked: "You need anything?"
"You bet! How 'bout a ride out of here!" called a young, sunburned and wet lady using socks for paddling gloves. Her face told me she was not having fun.
"We're in this for the long hual people! Remember?" the GUIDE shot back. And then he asked me: "You listened to the weather for day after tomorrow? Supposed to turn nasty and strong north winds," he said with a worried look.
"Yeah, well, we're headed for Willy Willy. Your best bet is to hole up in Rodgers River chickee or Indian Creek camp. They got protection from a northerly blow. I think lightnin' blasted the porta potti at the chickee, but I ain't sure 'bout that. See ya and good luck!" I yelled as we motored off.

Later, while offloading our gear, Gator asked me why I didn't suggest the canoeists head for Willy Willy since it was much closer.

"'Cause, friend, there was twelve of them, this's a small camp area and from the looks of it, the porta-potti has been very recently serviced. I need to say more?"
"Nope, nope. Hadn't thought a that. Good thinking."

After setting up camp, we set out to explore Rocky Creek. There are numerous freshwater creeks that feed the area and soon Ned called on the VHF to report hooking a gar. Gator was busy catching trout and I seemed to have cornered the market on voracious jacks .. fun to catch any day. But by mid-afternoon, I was sitting in the Rule #13, not casting, drowsy and wondering if those Coronas we tied to a mangrove root in the cool water were about right for drinking. I hailed Ned and Gator to advise them I was done for the day. The others were having too much fun catching fish and didn't respond.

When, eventually, they returned to camp they found me with feet up on the table bench and slouched comfortably in my canvas chair and trying to hold the weather radio up to catch a weather forecast. What I'd heard in between outbursts of static caused me to switch from creek cool beer to The Fisherman's Friend .. a jug of fine Barbados' rum.

"Whatchya hear, there, Stubb" asked Ned.

"Nothing good, fellas. Big norther blowin' in mid-afternoon tomorrow. Twenty knots and gusting to thrity, NNW. Gator'n I know from hard experience that kinda wind blows the water out of the back country and these skiffs aren't my choice fer headin' out to the Gulf Islands in that weather."
"Boy, that's right. I remember last March when we got caught. Hmm…them canoers'll make good time to Flamingo, though!" exclaimed Gator.

We talked it over during happy hour and dinner. We'd originally planned to stay in Willy two nights and then go on to Camp Lonesome. At the last moment, we'd changed our minds and reversed the plan figuring that we'd make the furthest camp from Chokoloskee Island on our itinerary, Camp Lonesome, then work our way back north to Willy Willy. As it turned out, given the forecast, we decided to cut the loop trip short by one night and not tempt the wind gods. Loaded as we were, our skiffs would only average 15-18 miles per hour. But we calculated we had enough time in the morning to fish some more, then push back to Choko and still beat the weather.

We almost didn't figure it right. About thirty minutes after loading our boats up at the Outdoor Resort ramp on Chokoloskee, and while answering questions about our catch from locally famous "Ranger John", the wind shifted sharply, clouds rolled in and a notable chill hit the air.

Ned looked up to the sky, sniffed the air, and said:

"We cut that almighty close, fellers. We'd left an hour or two later and it woulda been foul-weather gear and one hand to the bilge pump fer sure. Don't mind sayin' I'm glad that ain't the case. Our Willy Willy option was smart and we didn't know it."

The Wilderness at Low Water

Gator, Les and I gazed at two mini-skiffs, a Gheenoe Classic and an East Cape Glademen, loaded to the gunwhales with camping and fishing gear. Fortunately, both boats were beached on Chokoloskee Island. Their bows were high and dry because we weren't quite sure either one would float once we boarded and shoved off. Assuming, naturally, that the gear loads would let us "shove off." . If they would float, there were valid concerns about the amount of freeboard available to handle the fifteen knot NNW winds that lashed at the inland bays along the Wilderness Waterway.

"Hmmmm," mused Gator. "My tupperware tubs fit just right on the foredeck and behind the live well but I ain't sure but what I didn't bring a bit too much stuff."

"I keep telling you, Bubba, that all that water, ten gallons at eight pounds per gallon, is a lot excessive. A half gallon of rum would last you 4 days just fine and only weighs about a pound." Nobody responded to my comment, however, so I kept my thoughts to myself.

"Can you leave that tub behind?" asked Les and he pointed to the container full of tents, camp chairs, cook stove and cans of Beanie Weenie, Gator's version of emergency rations.

There was no reply to this outrage because, given our combined record of skunks, Beanie Weenie might constitute our first camping night's dinner .. if not night numbers two and three. So, with a glance to the low cloud cover and gusting winds, we grunted the bows off the bank, fired up the mighty 9.9 and 15 horse outboards, and galloped into the Turner River headed twenty miles SSE to Darwin's Place.

The plan was to meet with friends Vivian and Connie. They are confirmed yakeros and canoeists and had been mothershipped into the coastal 'Glades the day before by Captain Charles Wright of Everglades City. From Darwin's we would roam the small creeks and bays in all directions. You note I said "small creeks" and with good reason: the strong winds made the larger bays wildly choppy.

The two skiffs had no difficulty meandering the 20 odd miles to Darwin's. We only ran aground fifteen or twenty times, even using what we thought were good GPS tracks made on previous trips. We got turned around twice and ended up doing two tours of Crooked Creek; none of us noticed it until I sighted a dead mangrove I'd shot a picture of thirty minutes earlier. We stopped, conferred, consulted charts and GPS tracks, cussed each other out, and got headed in the right direction.

Eventually, we landed on Darwin's Place campsite. Viv and Connie, models of minimalist wilderness paddling, were set up: their tent tucked against a Gumbo Limbo tree; water in coon-proof containers hanging from tree limbs; canoes snugged up on high ground. We lumbered to a stop on the shell landing and were treated to loud, long and outraged comments from the ladies about the amount of gear we brought. However, knowing them as I do, I produced a genuine four cup coffee press and a freshly ground pound of Starbuck's Ethiopian Sidama coffee, and became an instant hero. My mama didn't raise a fool.

The next two days were ones of exploration coupled with fishing. And freezing! The sunrise showed the temps at forty degrees (Gator's infamous watch not only gives us altitude, barometric and humidity readings but also the temperature. I think it tells the time, too.). The strong winds kept us in the aforementioned creeks and we caught snook; few were keepers but they were of a size to make us happy. We ventured down one creek, poling, slogging through mud bars, and on into a series of large shallow bays. And the snook were in there! Smart, the snook were laid up in a foot of water and mud since the sun warms those areas up quickly. We didn't see them, until poling by, and it was like sight fishing redfish: a fin here, a tail there, a cast into the movement, a "whoa,,, got a hook up!" Dinner was assured.

There was a slight problem, however. Every evening, each morning, we'd look at the water level on the tiny shell beach where the skiffs and canoes rested, and noted something disturbing: the water level did not go up with tide changes. Strong northerly winds were stalling tidal surges. However, since to our eyes the surrounding levels were constant, we didn't worry about it much.

We should have been concerned.

Our last day at Darwin's Place had Les, Gator and I loading the skiffs back up; we eyeballed the water level again .. hadn't budged. Winds were still strong, to fifteen plus and gusting NNE, but "ho hum .. looks OK to me!" was the attitude. Viv and

Connie were to be picked up with their canoes by Captain Wright; no worries there, so we took off.

Details of the return trip would be tedious here. So, I'll summarize. In a mini-skiff running a 9.9 or 15 horse outboard, the trip from Chokoloskee Island to Darwin's, or the return, via the Wilderness Waterway, should not take more than an hour. Just coasting along, enjoying the scenerey. But, unknown to us, the water gauge at the mouth of the Turner River that day dropped off the graph. We got beat to death in Chevalier Bay by the chop; got detoured out of several creek passages that had gone dry; had to pole our way through the two Cross Bays; and pushed the skiffs out of Mud Shoal Bay. When we got to Chokoskee Bay .. there was no water!! I climbed an oyster bar to see if there were channels with water to get us to the launch ramp. The return trip took four hours .. but we made it.

Would I go back? Yes, but I'll have a pair of wading boots with me next time.

Just Folks

We all know these folks in the following pages. Oh, they have different names and appearances and are your family, not mine. But, you know'm.

In fact, there's no better way to really learn about folks than to be together on a boat in a blow; or, to be cooped up in a fish camp trailer during a tropical storm with half dozen other fishermen when the beer and rum starts flowing. That's when the word "personality" takes on new meaning.

Here's a few examples ...

THE BENDBACK BEADBUTT BAITFISH

AND OTHER STUFF

Most of my friends have converted to fly fishing these days and now they not only speak a different language but covet items like tippets, clousers, Tibor and Sage. All of which led to a conversation I had some time ago over at the launch ramp at Chokoloskee's Outdoor Resorts.

I was watching my friends FrenchFly, Jeremy, and AP carefully and cautiously taking their fly rods out of velvet lined cases and then fitting the rod pieces together by aligning little white dots. Now, I felt a bit conspicious getting my tackle out. All three of my rods and reels were just where I'd left them the weekend before: laying in the bed of the pickup. I've learned if I don't leave the rigs there I'll forget to bring them at o'dark thirty in the morning. I didn't have any velvet lined rod cases and now I'm used to the green tint of salt tarnish on the reels.

AP had his rod cradled like a newborn in the crook of his arm, everything put together, line ready to his satisfaction, and was thinking out loud about his fly selection for the morning:

"Think I'm not ready for a shootin' head, today. Hmmm, maybe this will work."

And he began performing a complicated knot trick on a fly with a hook hidden by bunny fur and other flashy stuff.

"What's that, AP?" French asked. "One a your Clousers? A Sexy Slider?"

"No sir. This's a genu-wine home made BendBack Beadbutt Baitsfish. Guaranteed to whistle up leapin' tarpon, lurkin' gator trout and bull reds."

Within seconds every fly wander within hearing had gathered round to examine AP's work. I strolled over as well. I liked the fly's name even though I knew nothing about it. I'm not sure what I expected;

however, what lay in his hand wasn't it. I looked and asked:

"Where's the "beadbutt" AP? Don't see it."

"Stubb, it's all in the handiwork and design. This,you see, is called finesse fishin'."

"You sayin' my spinnin' gear lacks finesse?"

"Yup. Thought I said it pretty clear, didn't I?"

"Well," I whipped back, never one to leave things hanging, "You showed a bunch of finesse the last couple years breakin', by your own admission, at least five high dollar fly rods. And, if I recall correctly, this rod replaces the latest one busted."

"Not my fault!" protested AP loudly and with eyes bugged wide. "That mangrove literally snatched the Sage right outta my hand! I was lucky to salvage the reel and line!"

"A fierce struggle with that tree, I'm sure, AP. Can't trust them mangroves at all."

Although I'd given AP a hard time about a militant rod grabbing mangrove, I have to admit I've lost a similar battle or two in times past; but I wasn't going to admit that at the moment. A verbal skirmish about tackle with fishing friends is about as much fun as actually catching fish, in my opinion, and I hurried off to get on the water before he could make a come-back.

Some weeks later, down on Chokoloskee Island, the same group was gathered on the covered porch of our rental trailer. The wind was blowing nearly thirty knots and carried with it a frog strangler rain. By noon, the weather didn't look to clear soon and the beer began to flow, all of which assisted deep philosophical discussions about Life, the Universe and Everything in General.

AP dragged out his portable fly tie gear and was busily snipping, gluing, and talking. We were joined by our temporary next door neighbor, Toby the Knifemaker, who was at the point of enjoying himself despite the foul weather. The talk topics ran the usual and finally settled on the delicate balance between fishing and maintaining a marriage. Toby said:

"Got lucky w' the last lady. She run off with a trucker otherwise it'd a been life without parole for me."

"You're single, Stubb, you wouldn't understand all this." Opined Gator. But I replied:

"Wrong. My first wife hated boats, the water and all such. After we split up the first guy she took up with owned a thirty foot sailboat and she loved it."

"Well, I been married for …? Hmm, twenty odd years now," mused AP."Been pretty good but the wife, she's not an outdoorsy type. Never was. How's this fly look, fellas? OK? But, as I was sayin', she's never quite understood my devotion to all things fishin', understand? Why, when I told her about this here trip, five days, she just looked at me and shook her head and said: 'I thought it was just a weekend! Five days? Do you *have* to fish?'"

And, AP stood up and started pacing as he related this, using his hands like an orator:

"'Do you *have* to fish?' she asked me." AP looked down and shook his head up and down emphatically: "'Yes!' I told her absolutely; 'yes!'" He struggled for words a moment and stared at all of us on the porch and:

"So, a third time I said 'yes!' and pretty much left it at that and kept on packin'."

AP sat back down to finish his tie job and his cell phone rang.

He answered: "Oh, hi, honey. Nah. Rained us out today. I'm just finishin' up a Bendback Beadbutt Baitfish. Looks fine." He was quiet, listening a minute, then said:

"I don't know, but I figure that bit of fur you cut off your old mink coat will do the trick and this fly will finally catch somethin."

(Author's note: Is this a Bendback Beadbutt Baitfish? Well, I haven't a clue but AP swears it's a picture of his version. I'll let the fly wand wavers haggle about it all.)

Dog Days Chickee Fishing

The fifteen horse outboard burbled at slow forward idle speed as my mini-skiff, The Rule #13, crept into the marina on Chokoloskee Island. There was so little breeze that August noon the humidity simply settled over your head and created a hazy cloud that followed you around. French and I were burned, sweated out and, importantly, completely skunked for the morning. Oh, we'd had shots at snook, some slashing hits and near thing misses, but nothing brought to the boat.

After securing the skiff and staggering up the moss slick wood ladder to the dock, we dragged ourselves to the shade of the chickee and collapsed into porch swings surrounded by our rods, tackle and empty water bottles.

"Flip coins to see who'll go to the trailer and get ice cold beers?" I offered as I fished a quarter out of my pocket.
"Nah," said French. "I couldn't see the coin, eyes 're too blurry and besides you'd just cheat."
"Whattaya mean by that?" I squalled. "I wouldn't do that… er, well, I might, though."

After we argued over who'd walk the entire one hundred fifty feet to the trailer for cold ones, French gave up and disappeared into the haze. I could tell he was walking away since the sound of his Crocs slapping the tarmac got fainter while I started to doze.

The early morning started out well enough; we'd loaded up and zipped into the maze of islets just west of the island taking advantage of the swift outgoing tides. We drifted along fishing near the mangroves, casting at ambush points where snook and other predators might lurk, and making derogatory comments on each other's casting ability. About one cast in five snagged a mangrove requiring a retrieval laced with cussing the glue-like quality of aquatic plant life. I was using a suspending, three inch hard plug, that previously snook and trout found to be irresistible. French, as always, manned the foredeck so he could practice the fine art of fly fishing. I'm never sure what type fly the wand wavers use: to me it sounded like French was casting something called a "bowser" and at other times a "hurple burble marabou."

"Nice cast, French. You put the fly up ten foot 'bove the high tide mark."

"Yeah, well, you left at least two a them high dollar lures further up back in the last creek," grumbled French. "'Spensive day fer you, huh?"

And so it went all morning. We bickered and teased each other as we flailed our way through sloughs and bayous and exhausted the trolling motor battery and our casting arms. Unsurprisingly, it rained on us twice; there was no wind, just rain enough to soak us and create a personal steam bath where we stood in the skiff.

"Whose idea was it to come down here in August?" I wondered out loud. "There's not 20 people in residence on the island this month. All got better sense than us!"

"Was your idea, if you recall," mumbled French as he unwrapped his fly line that was twisted around his toes.

So, there was little joy in Choko land that afternoon in the chickee; however, enough of a breeze showed up to dry the sweat and keep the beer from boiling in the bottles.

As we sat there, two youngsters came clattering through the chickee carrying a rod each and a baggie full of shrimp. One of them lost a flip-flop and tripped on the gravel and fell sprawling on the dock. He squawked but not over any injury .. he was concerned about the spilled shrimp. Most of the bait was recovered and they plopped shrimp and popping corks into the marina basin that bubbled with an incoming tide. Promptly, both hooked a snook in the twenty five inch size. French and I just stared.

"I got a bloody finger from stripping fly line; eyes are burned out from the sun; and layin' here alongside me is a thousand bucks worth of rod and reel; and kids with half busted rigs're right in front a me catchin." French was outraged but too weary to say it too loudly.

"Be back in a minute," he said and lurched off into the sun.

He came back, collapsed in a chair alongside of mine and snatched up one of my spinning rigs, cut off the plug, and tied on a #2 hook and impaled a shrimp on it. I was speechless.

"What're you doin'?" I asked.
"Wuzit look like? Gonna catch me a fish or know the reason why. Them boys can do it, so can the Frenchman, by damn….." and he kept mumbling

half to himself as he scooted a lawn chair to the edge of the chickee shade and made a long cast into the marina waters.
"You touched a spinning rod!?? Where's my camera .. I gotta record this. Done backslid into the darkside at last, huh?"
"Shuttup and get me another beer," was the only response I got.

I ran to the RV, grabbed a camera and a six pack and surprised myself by being able to sprint back to the chickee without having heat stroke. When I got there I heard a whoop from French and the two boys. All three were hooked up. The boys got their fish in but French was having a wrestling match with his. The snook would zig toward a piling; French would muscle him back, all the while keeping his shady seat. The fight seesawed back and forth for two or three minutes until finally, Mr. Snook found the right barnacle encrusted piling and "snap-ziiing" went the leader.

French collapsed back into his chair, he'd been sitting on the edge of it but never stood up nor got out of the shade, and he dropped the spinning rig beside him.

His eyes were closed and I got suddenly worried:
"You all right?"
"No."
"Well, I got a picture of you fightin' that snook....."
"Well, wonderful," he replied with eyes still closed.
"Wanna see the pic?"
"No."
"Want another beer?"
"Yes."

"You gonna be like this all day?"
"Yes."
"You givin' up fly fishing?"

French turned and glared at me and started to say something, but a loud thunderclap boomed out and a frog strangler rain came at us horizontally. We were both soaked within seconds but it never occurred to us to move.

42 Degrees in the Shade

Ever since I started playing around in the 10,000 Islands and coastal Everglades, relating tales of remote campsites, running out of gas in the middle of nowhere, "discovering" Calusa shell mounds and having giant snook bust my tackle in little isolated bays, my parents have been curious about the place. However, it seemed unlikely that they'd get a chance to see the area given they live in Dallas, far far away, and on their yearly visits to New Smyrna Beach, the family sticks fairly close to Mosquito Lagoon.

My mother and father are life long waterfolk. Dad will tell you that he's forgotten how many boats he's owned. Mother will tick them off her fingers, however, one by one, and give you the size of the engine and the specs of each boat. The family has many memories of camping and fishing in the Kiamichi Mountains of southwestern Oklahoma, the forested hills of southeast Missouri, the swampy lakes and bayous of deep east Texas and Louisiana.

In fact, one of my earliest memories is laying in the bottom of Dad's 14' fiberglass over wood skiff with a towel stretched gunwhale to gunwhale for shade. That boat, with the "newfangled" thing called fiberglass, was a wonder in it's day. The motor, a 10hp Wizard, was a "crank and go" having neither neutral nor reverse. You had to be pointed in the right direction and give it Hell. Then they started getting bigger and better boats, aluminum and glass, Chris Craft cruisers (try keeping up the varnish on a mahogany hull!), then the earliest models of bass boats. Those rigs resemble the Gheenoes of today down to and including joy stick steering.

But, let's get back to the present. The folks are now in their mid-eighties, spry enough but jumping from docks to boat decks and facing the elements is much more of challenge than it was in 1948, 1955 or even 1980. However, last week, on a whim, I called friend Captain Charles Wright of Everglades City to see if he had a half day charter available. Fish or sight seeing, I didn't care. We'd whistle down the highway on Sunday morning, board one of his fleet of boats on Monday, return to New Smyrna on Monday evening.

Since Captain Wright has a kayak mothership (a 27' Carolina skiff designed to carry 6 kayaks and passengers comfortably) and does "livery service" wherein he will drop a yakero deep into the 'Glades then pick them up, and since this past Monday he had seats available, I packed up the folks and off we went.

It was a fairly ominous start to the trip. The first major cold front of the year blew in on December 16th. Winds started out that Sunday out of the south at 25 knots, heavy squalls, a tornado in Paso County, and watching to the west from our third floor balcony we saw walls of rain marching across Mosquito Lagoon's Cedar Island. Within an hour, it blew over. We loaded up the truck and headed south.

We rented a small park model cabin in Everglades City for the night; then munched grouper fingers and French fries at the City Market overlooking the Barron River. The wind had already turned to the north and as we ate I mentally went over our cold weather gear for the morning ride through the 'Glades. Let's see: three layers of clothes, couple of heavy jackets, no gloves, ball caps .. that's it.

Monday morning dawned bright and clear and colder than you might think Everglades City could get. Naples TV said the wind chill was 42 degrees with a NNW 12-15 knots, building to 20 in the afternoon. I had my doubts but we sucked down some coffee at 7 a.m. and drove to Captain Wright's place.

The good captain's wife provided gloves and ear muffs for the folks; we watched several groups of yakeros take off for the Gulf Islands, and observed our fellow passenger, a tiny lady of sixty six years called Michaeleen, load her gear on the mothership.

She was going on a five day solo kayak trip from the drop off, at Darwin's Place camp site, then to Lostman's River and return to Everglades City.

Despite the chill, even with experienced charter captains standing around in thermal gear, the folks were enthralled with it all. They talked with Michaeleen all during the ride to Darwin's Place, admired the scenery, the wildness, remote beauty and twisty turny roundy bout "who knows where we are" amazement that all newcomers experience with the coastal 'Glades.

I think the cold got to them but they never complained nor did anything but look and smile then thank the skipper and his friendly wife Vickie upon our return. I hope the trip was a great late life adventure for them. I know that every time I leave the docks in Chokoloskee or Everglades City, there's a gripping in my gut that tells me: "this place sets me on the edge of my seat."

And, on the return trip, highballing up Highways 29 and 70 and then I-95, Dad said: "Interesting place; but it was damned cold out there. Gereva? Remember when we owned that old Harkey boat and were up in Arkansas? In '50 or '51 ....??"

Small Craft Maintenance

Anyone who knows me will assure you that I am no mechanic at all. Back when I sold boats, I learned how to do some basic things with inboards and diesels the hard way. If you can bust your knuckles on any item, I'm the guy to show you how to do that.

But, my ineptitude has never stopped me from trying and once in a while I get it right. My rule here is that if a maintenance job is supposed to take one hour, I add forty eight to that which is how long it'll be for me to haul the boat to the right mechanic.

Small Craft Maintenance

Part I

The other evening I was underneath my outdoor stairwell busily pulling a poison oak vine off my kayak rudder. I gave a big yank on the vine, stumbled back into the wheel fender of my mini-skiff trailer, knocked off the tail light, bounced sideways, grabbed a poling platform stanchion, and then caromed around the boat transom and into my new outboard's propeller. I landed on my rear end, my breath whacked out of me, and decided not to move for a while. A neighbor and her two kids out for a walk applauded in appreciation ("Kin ya do that again mister?"). Unable to speak, I just glared and the lady gave a 'humph' and stalked off down the alley.

(Rule #13 loaded for an Everglades loop trip.)

Well, I needed gas for the tanks, and oil, so I figured I'd pick up a new tail light having mangled the one I dislodged. These errands run, I returned to do the five minute tail light fix. However, things don't always work out well, you know what I mean? Since that was the third light in a year, and I'd cut and spliced with great abandon, now the wires were too short. I couldn't locate any wire in my stash of "stuff," so I jumped in the truck to head back to the store. It was right then I noticed one of the empty oil containers I'd bought and poured into one of my two gas tanks. The container looked wrong. Ooops. Wrong oil! It wasn't two cycle. I'd bought two different types of oil and used both. But, which tank had the wrong oil?

Now, friends, you might want to say: "It's OK, Stubb. Just dump the gas/oil mix and do it over again." Easy but not my style. In the first place, I'd no "where" nor no "thing" into which I could place the suspect mix. Never mind that six gallons of gas at current prices nagged at me. And, pouring the mix into the shell and sand parking area where I live wasn't an option. I didn't need the lot on fire. More importantly, however, I was protective of my brand new fifteen horse Johnson and wasn't about to mess with half measures.

I recalled that the corner store, Sanjay's Quik Stop, also had an outdoor oil change facility. Sanjay is a friendly soul and sells everything from cell phones and gas to ginseng and he had used oil storage. He was surprised to see me back so soon after gassing up and I told him the gas wouldn't work in the boat. I needed to dump it.

"I have no demons in my gas, sir!"
"I know that, Sanjay, I mistakenly added a potential demon to the gas .. that's why I'll pay you to take it back." I explained. But Sanjay was now wary:
"I don't need any demons, thank you, sir!"

Well, it took a while but I finally made him understand and he charged me $20 to dispose of the demon possessed gas and oil. He did give me a nickel per gallon discount on a new fill up. Even better, he rummaged around in his back room and found me the right size tail light wire which he also discounted. Somehow, a dollar a foot sounded excessive and not much of a discount but I only needed a foot or so and I wasn't in the mood to haggle.

Alright! I'm back home around $60 poorer and ready to replace the tail light. I couldn't find my wire stripper so I used my super sharp multi-tool knife and sliced my thumb to the bone. It took two shop rags to hold the blood flow and get me the few blocks to the ER. I asked for sedatives while the doctor stitched me up, but the doctor cocked an eyebrow and declined the prescription.

"How'd you do this, Mr Stubblefield?" he asked as he stitched.
"I was pulling a poison oak vine off my kayak ruder, and ..."
"Hmm. Poison oak? That would explain this rash and swelling on your neck, arm and other hand, " the doctor mumbled.
"I was using gloves!!"

"But when you cut yourself you used a knife. How's an oak vine fit into this…?"

I gave up on the explanation as it was too involved.

The doc did say to keep the bandage clean and dry and recommended no trailer repairs nor fishing that weekend. I advised him that was not giving me much customer satisfaction which remark fazed him not at all. So, loaded down with a bag of lotion for my neck, arm and good hand, I went back home. I sat up on the balcony overlooking the boat and kayak, favoring my slit thumb, and pondered my options which were as follows:

1. Supposed to keep this thumb clean and dry. Use a glove, obviously, when fishing.
2. Reel handling? I'm left handed which means I can't reel with my injured right hand while retrieving .. not easily at any rate. Solution? Reverse the reel handle. Done.
3. Trailer tail lights? Hey, it's day time, isn't it? The Rule #13 (my skiff) is small and the truck lights are seeable. No problem.

Within minutes I'd donned a glove, reversed the handles of two reels and hooked up the skiff and was driving through the neighborhood. I coasted through a stop sign, accelerated and then noticed the flashing lights right behind me.

The cop was polite enough although he had several pointed questions about why I didn't have trailer lights; why I didn't come to a full stop "back yonder;" what did I do to get a busted thumb; why was my neck, arm and good hand swole up; and how come it was I towed a trailer with a flat tire.

He let me off with a warning on most of the infractions but did give me a $75 ticket for failure to use the seat belt. My protest that hooking the belt with a bandage the size of a cucumber cut no ice. He escorted me the eight blocks home, since the flat tire caused me to drive very slowly. I'd not gotten around to mounting a spare on the trailer.

I never did get to the saltwater that day. And, I've been meaning to air up that tire.

SMALL CRAFT MAINTENANCE
Part II
(Graphical Arts)

There we were on a kerosene stove hot, late summer's day, standing around gazing at trucks, boats and trailers at a Tamiami Trail dirt ramp. We were comparing rigs and gear, sipping no longer cool drinks and ignoring the fact that not a single fella in three boats had even snag hooked a game fish that morning. Naturally, the discussion turned to the proper appearance of a flats skiff and my little boat was undergoing some intense scrutiny by the assembled critics:

"Stubb, you gotta fix up yer boat name. Looks raggedy," said Gator as he swatted blindly at no-see-ums. "Color's all wrong and it don't stand out, much, you know. It's got no style."

"Yeah," chimed in The FrenchFly. "Lookee here .. these letters're startin' to peel off. See? I can grab this '3' real easy.." and by golly he was removing the number which would transform my skiff, the "Rule #13" to the "Rule #1." There were signifcant metaphysical reasons for the boat's name and I was outraged.

"Hey, hey, there, hold on….! Them'll last a while longer 'n besides, skins 'n bumps, nicks 'n such give her a salty look," I said as I wet my thumb and tried to get the top half of the "3" to stick back to the fiberglass.

This announcement was met with cackles and heehaws and several remarks about maybe needing to drop the skiff off the trailer while doing seventy miles per hour to give it "jist a bit more salt." It was well known that some years back, and very near this same spot, I'd forgotten to tie down my kayak to the truck and thereby learned that plastic craft will fly at least one hundred feet given the right launch technique and speed. This event was witnessed by a terrified family of Michiganders who were tailgating me. We were all amazed at the lack of big damage.

All the way home that afternoon I thought about dressing up my rig and I got the kind of expensive help fishing friends push your way. Gator emailed me a link to a boat graphics company and he suggested some sample fonts, colors and styles. And, as if I needed to be shoved in the right direction, he included several pictures of our friends' boat graphics. Foremost among those pictures was one of his "Gatorbait." The email assured me the process would take an hour and would make the "Rule #13" truly stand out.

So, $99 later, I had my sets of registration numbers and boat names, with five pages of detailed instructions. I decided, for once in my life, to actually sit down to read and examine the items that came with the graphics before slapping them on the hull. Since the instructions came in fourteen languages and it was well into Happy Hour, several minutes went by before I realized I was trying to read Portuguese. Then I found "English" and got down to it.

Hmmm. A squeegee, special soap, mineral spirits, latex gloves, and a safety razor. I assumed the razor was for slashing your wrists if the graphics got futzed up and I was correct, but more on that another time. And, it said, again in fourteen languages, "…improper set of graphicals may result in premature degradation…" Or, I thought, extreme exasperation and despair.

I sat back and pondered the whole deal. "Stubb, you've watched guys pinstripe cars and boats before and they did it in about a flash. Wonder if I could hire one 'a them dudes do this?"

Anyway, the next day was not perfect for "proper set of graphicals" in that it was muggy, cloudy, drizzling every now and then, and with a heat index off the thermometer. But, I was determined and got to it. Now, I haven't room here to give step by step processes of the ordeal, er .. I mean application; but, suffice it to say that even though Gator and the instructions allowed one hour for completion, it took me nearly six.

Fortunately, I was ably assisted by two curious neighbors with a large supply of cold beer and advice. I managed to get the hull clean, wax-free; only had to remove slick, wet "graphicals" five times (they were crooked and suffered from bubble-itis); squeegeed as instructed; and, importantly, didn't have to slash my wrists with the thoughtfully provided safety razor.

A week later on a sweltering pre-dawn morning, I rolled into Everglades City; hopped out and strutted over to the group of friends drinking bad coffee and smearing themselves with bug juice. I was in a fine mood and, unlike most of the guys, got a solid night's sleep. And, I especially wanted to show off my new boat graphics. I was rather proud of the job, you see.

"Mornin', mornin', how's everbody? Lookit my new boat name!"

"Humph," muttered FrenchFly, chin sinking down to his chest, he was four fifths alseep.

"Stubb, you got the 'FL' too far from the numbers here on the starboard side," Gator said as he belched.

"Yeah, an' you shoulda ordered'm bigger. Maybe a simpler style," and several other similar remarks followed before my fishing friends lost interest as the bait truck pulled up.

Well, some one famous once said that critics are a dime a dozen. If that's true then I've got a buck's worth.

SMALL CRAFT MAINTENANCE
PART III

(Essential Accessories)

I think we all lose sight of the fact that boats, whatever their size or design, firstly, are made to keep you on top of the water and thereby save you from drowning; and, secondly (hopefully), to get you from one place to another on the water in semi-dry condition. You note I said "semi-dry" and did not mention blood or the physical manifestations of sea-sickness which may render the mariner damp and miserable; but, nevertheless, he lived to crawl to dry land again.

In my own case, as chronicled in earlier articles, my mini-flats skiff, The Rule #13, has not failed to get me there and back again. Yet, there were some items I deemed necessary after months of trial, error and terror. For example, despite the fact it's not wise to motor a small boat while standing, I do it in order to get a better idea of the shallows, sand and oyster bars. I run a small outboard with a long tiller extension. But one day, zipping along in Mosquito Lagoon's "east channel," I was introduced to a sand bar that I would swear was built up in the past week. Hitting it at full tilt boogie didn't hurt the boat or motor but ended up catapaulting me forward to where I had a bear hug on the trolling motor.

This event was witnessed by a couple of friends, Gator and The FrenchFly, who expressed a great deal of concern for my safety, they claimed, between fits of laughter and giggles.

"Stubb! We's afraid you were killed (snort, chuckle)!"

"I may be done for; I'm afraid to stand up," I replied while unwinding myself from the foredeck. "You, my man, need a grab bar n' maybe a cushion tied down near the bow."

A grab bar? Hmmm. The very thing: handy, stylish, good safety item, you can hang dongles from it, plus it looks salty. I'm afraid the "salty" part sold me after I checked out a boat here and there that had such grab bars. Anyhow, I drew up some plans, found an aluminum welding shop, and had it made. I installed it myself and am pleased to report I suffered no serious injuries handling drills, screw drivers and mounting hardware. The result looks good (see below) and I've already put it to the test down near Chokoloskee where I located my 394th oyster bed some fifty feet from the launch ramp.

However, I wasn't done at all. You can see that my little skiff has a poling platform (see previous page). It was designed by my friend Tacklehead who originally bought the rig. He found a welder up in the north Georgia mountains who'd never seen a poling platform but nevertheless gave it a shot. The result was good, but, the details of the construct left something to be desired. It was too low for the new motor I added requiring you to turn the motor port or starboard to tilt it up; the low profile meant I stripped the skin off my hand numerous times pulling the starter rope; plus, after adding the grab bar with it's elegant one inch tubing, the square stock of the platform looked rather, well, crummy.

I consulted various websites, looking at designs. I spoke with most of my fishing friends and got dubious advice. Tacklehead, who's moved up to a fine looking 17' flats boat, had a "forward of the engine" platform put on his rig. He explained at great and tedious length:

"See, Stubb, that means the weight's forward which helps when fishin' by yerself. An', the platform can be shorter, more stable an' don't interfere w'the motor tiltin' up an' all that stuff."

"But," I replied, "on my boat I'd be sitting under the platform; she's not big enough for that. Also, instead of just gettin' wet if you fall off it, now you have a good chance of landin' on the motor, crackin' your ribs and, given your weight, bustin' the cowling."

"I ain't gonna fall off, Stubb an' I'll have you know I dropped thirty pound lately."

Then I chanced upon a flats skiff, I forget the brand, but it was about an eighteen footer, with a tall "over the motor" platform. Pretty standard, yes. But welded to that was an aluminum waist high cage of sorts that enclosed the poler on 3 sides. It looked immense!!

While I was gazing at the boat, assessing the pros and cons, an old man walked up from the shoreline where he'd beached his battered jon boat. He said:

"Feller could hang hisself with that thing."
"Whatcha mean? How?" I was trying to figure out his statement, you see.
"See that there lanyard he's got dangling off the back rest? Why, if'n it got a bit rough, wetted down the platform deck, an' he slips, as he's goin' down could git caught in it and whoosh .. deader'n a stump." He laughed to himself, shook his head, and walked away.

Since I'm a walking injury magnet, the double platform was out of the question. And, I liked the square footage of my existing platform which gave me enough room to actually take a step sideways; a significant advantage according to Gator.

"Stubb, lookit my platform. It fits the boat but I got about four inches beyond my size thirteen shoes. I can't get excited up there an' shuffle around or I could take a dive!"

That convinced me. I called the guys who made my grab bar and had them take the existing top and deck mounts, knock off the square stock legs, and weld on that nice, graceful tubing.

I'm done with the boat, now. It's got everything it needs. I didn't think that was the case until I added up the cost of essential accessories. They cost more than the original hull.

Character(s)

One day a few years ago an acquaintance, having read one of my articles, took me to task. He advised me I'd not exactly related an event as it happened nor had I gotten the brief conversations word for word. My response was:

"Have I represented the folks in the piece accurately? Have I insulted you? Would you call it libel or character assassination? If so, here's my attorney's name and number..."

And I gave him the number for the state prison in Raiford and a name I dreamed up.

I never saw or heard from the fella again so I suppose nothing will come of it. However, one genuine legal type did tell me I should acknowledge those I so liberally quote just to keep them happy (or quiet, maybe). I was a bit outraged but then, after some thought, I decided I'd do it and put snapshots alongside their names.

So, I called the cast of characters and told them what I was up to. Imagine my surprise when I heard some hesitation. It went something like this:

"Er, Stubb, now .. lemme think. Mebbe just my nickname, OK? After all, I'm not sure BettyLou (or substitute the correct wife's name) knows I was out doin' and goin' that day. I doubt she'd ever read it, you know? But I don't need any trouble 'round here since I wrecked the pickup after I ran over her cat...."

Well, fine. So, here's a few snapshots with the nicknames of the intrepid fisherfolk only. However, I suspect "BettyLou" knows full well where so and so was and when .. he's got not the least idea….

In no particular order:

NMZ (No Motor Zone) Ned

AP (The Rodbuster)

French (The FrenchFly)

Gator (a.k.a Gadgethead)

Yours Truly (a.ka. Stubb, Fishslayer .. sigh.. I wish)

There are others but they declined the honor of having their picture published. They are:

Half Naked Charlie: he's hiding out down in Belize I'm told.

Tacklehead: Now engaged to a mysterious lady and denies all knowledge of his past life.

Les (a.ka. The Mess): in exile in South Dakota; but I got him in a picture nonetheless .. see "Lostman's Luck"

www.ingramcontent.com/pod-product-compliance
Lightning Source LLC
Chambersburg PA
CBHW020015050426
42450CB00005B/478